how to HEAL

MIKE NOVOTNY

Published by Straight Talk Books
P.O. Box 301, Milwaukee, WI 53201
800.661.3311 • timeofgrace.org

Printed in the United States of America
ISBN: 978-1-949488-43-2

Contents

Introduction

Over the years, God has taught me a simple equation for personal restoration: Healing = Bible + People.

When someone has been through a traumatic event—an unexpected death, a painful divorce, a loved one's addiction, etc.—few things have the power to heal quite like God's Word and God's people. Keeping secrets keeps us stuck in our pain, but humbly opening the Word and inviting others into our lives has healing power that I can't quite explain.

Or maybe I can explain it . . .

"When anxiety was great within me, [God's] **consolation brought me joy"** (Psalm 94:19).

"Pray for each other so that you may be healed" (James 5:16).

That restoration equation is the reason why I have spent three entire Sundays addressing the issue of abuse in my church and on *Time of Grace*, bringing this taboo topic out of the darkness and into the light of our conversations. What a season of healing it has been! Every message has been met with a flurry of texts and emails from hurting believers who have experienced healing from God's mighty yet tender hand.

It's beautiful.

That's why I'm so glad you are reading this book. Perhaps you love someone dearly who has endured the trauma of abuse. Perhaps you want to be an ally to help others with their healing. Perhaps you are humble enough to realize that you have patterns of abusive behavior in your own life. Or perhaps you yourself are dealing with the wounds from your past. Whatever your situation, I hope the restoration equation produces something beautiful in you and something powerful through you.

On the following pages, you'll find chapters under the

heading: "Abuse: What Does God Say?" These chapters look at what God says to the abused, the abusive, and to his people of the church. Then you'll find a series of devotions based on those three chapters. You'll notice that some of the content in the devotions is the same as parts of the previous chapters, but the intent is to take you deeper into God's Word, to give you a chance to reflect on his Word and learn from it, to jot down your thoughts, and to pray. In addition, you will find some of the responses that I received after beginning this delicate conversation. Names, details, and specifics have been altered, of course, since confessions are personal and the trust of our church is something that I treasure. In the case of any extended quotes, express permission was given for me to share with you.

I hope this book, filled with God's Word and God's people, brings our Father's healing touch to your heart.

"Gracious words are a honeycomb, sweet to the soul and healing to the bones" (Proverbs 16:24).

Abuse: What Does God Say to the Abused?

When our church (The CORE) first opened in an old movie theatre, our congregation decided to put three massive words on the side of the building—*Real. Relevant. Relational.* Those words were more than a trendy tagline; they were our hope and our prayer, what we wanted in our DNA. We wanted the church to be real. Even if "real" was raw and messy and complicated and uncomfortable, we wanted to talk about real life and real issues and real struggles. Because real is relevant. All of us do stuff and deal with stuff that isn't neat and tidy and churchy, stuff that we need help with and forgiveness for. And we wanted it to be relational, a church where you wouldn't have to fake it or hide it but could confess it and deal with it together. When I became the main speaker for Time of Grace, I wanted to be sure to be real, relevant, and relational to that audience as well as my home congregation. That's why we had a series called *Gay & God* and another on race and God and another on God and gender. A series called *Taboo* covered depression, suicide, and drinking. Another covered porn and still another dating and divorce. But there's something I've barely mentioned in all these years. That something is . . . abuse.

The complexity of addressing abuse, honestly, scares me. I'm scared that if I stay silent, some of you will continue to get hurt and others of you won't heal. And I'm scared that if I break the silence, some of you will get hurt or my words might trigger old trauma. I'm scared of being so generic you don't see the many forms abuse takes. Talking abuse is like walking a tightrope, especially for an average pastor like me. So I just want to say that if I slip up, when I slip up, when the words aren't just right, when I miss the mark, I need you to know my heart is to help. I need to be real because so many people can relate, and they need a relationship with God, with you and me, to move forward. I know this is not easy, but it is good for us to talk about abuse.

Because abuse happens a lot. According to the National Domestic Violence Hotline (thehotline.org), abuse is a pattern of behavior that uses fear and force to maintain power and control. This isn't one-time name-calling but a pattern of behavior. It's not just physical force but also psychological fear—an assault on your mental well-being. And abuse's goal is control. Abusers want to get their own way, so they do whatever it takes to get it. He slaps a face, punches a wall, kicks a pet, and controls the cash. She degrades with insults, isolates from friends, touches without consent. They blow up, blow off a blowup, blame you for a blowup, threaten to take the kids, threaten to hurt themselves. Abusers even twist Scripture—"You have to submit to me"; "You have to forgive me"; "Love keeps no record of wrongs, so you can't call the cops"; "If you honored your father, you wouldn't; if you loved your mother, you'd never." They do whatever it takes to make you do what they want.

All of that happens a lot. According to the Centers for Disease Control and Prevention (cdc.gov), 1 in 4 women and 1 in 7 men have experienced severe physical abuse in their lives. That's just physical. And that means abuse affects you and me—men and women, brothers and sisters, us. If 300 people come to my church on Sunday, 150 men and 150 women, 59 of them have endured/will endure severe physical violence. On an average Sunday, by those same odds, 59,000 people watching *Time of Grace* have been through it too. 59,000! Abuse is real and relevant and affects our relationships.

Given the complexity of it all, I want to spend the next three chapters talking to three specific groups of people. In this first chapter, I want to speak to people who have been abused. Next, to the abusers themselves. Finally, to everyone who knows one or the other. I know those overlap, that the abused can become abusive, which is why I hope you will read all three chapters. Our precious souls need to heal. So let's start by looking into God's Word and addressing those who have experienced abuse.

One of my most vivid memories of dealing with abuse is from a few years ago. A man came to our church and was excited about growing in his faith. But one day he confessed to me that he had hurt his girlfriend. He was wrecked by his angry behavior, weeping and sorry for what he had done. (After our conversation, I called a cop from church and asked what I should do with such information, but he said lamentably that the woman needed first to make a charge.) Before the abuser left my office, however, I told him what I would tell any sinner who was truly sorry. I told him that Jesus died for us; that Jesus died even for this; that even though there would be earthly consequences, Jesus could save him from condemnation. I even texted him a Bible passage afterward about God's grace. Later, however, I would come to regret that text. Because weeks later, the woman showed up at my office and told me the rest of the story. She gave me the details of how physical the physical abuse was, details that broke my heart, and then she revealed what her boyfriend had done with my text. "See," he shoved his phone in her face. "The pastor is on my side. God is on my side." I have never felt so angry and so sorry at the same time. That experience helped me see abuse up close—how muddied a manipulator can make things. That's why I want to open the Bible and be perfectly clear about what God thinks of abuse.

Let's start with this: *God hates abuse.* Highlight that and remember it. God hates abuse. In this broken world, we often wonder why God doesn't just stop bad stuff from happening. His timing and his plans confuse us and make us question what he thinks about our pain. But this much is clear—God hates abuse. Here are three passages to prove it: **"So God said to Noah, 'I am going to put an end to all people, for the earth is filled with violence because of them'"** (Genesis 6:13). Remember Noah and the ark and the flood? Why did God do that? Because of abuse. Because violent force replaced humble faith, and God could not stand it. And neither could Jesus: **"If anyone causes one of these little ones—those who believe in me—to stumble, it would be better for them to have a large millstone hung around their neck and to be drowned in the depths of the sea"** (Matthew 18:6). If you mislead a child, damage a child, use and confuse a child, cause them to stumble and struggle for your own power and pleasure, it would be better to have a large millstone—not even a regular one but a large one!—hung around your neck to drown you. Because God hates abuse. God hates it when anyone uses their size and strength and their authority or position to hurt a child. But maybe this psalm says it best: **"The Lord examines the righteous, but the wicked, those who love violence, he hates with a passion"** (11:5). God doesn't just hate violence. He hates those who love violence. And he doesn't just hate them. He hates them with a passion.

If you have or are abusing someone, you need to keep reading and also read the next chapter (there is hope for you too!), but if you have been abused, let these words cut through all the garbage your abuser piled up to hide the truth. God hates abuse. Every time. God never minimizes it or justifies it. God never, ever says it's okay because he was drunk or because she was stressed. He doesn't blame it on you. It's not your fault. You are not responsible, no matter what they say. Please hear me.

It breaks our Father's heart when abuse happens because God hates abuse.

Second, *God loves the abused.* A few years back, a wise pastor told me about the funny way our minds do math. He had just read a study that said when one person says something to you ten times and ten people say something to you one time, our brains feel about the same. 1x10 = 1+1+1+1+1+1+1+1+1+1. In other words, it only takes one constant critic or one abusive voice to overwhelm your mind. So if your mom or your boyfriend says, "You're so dumb. You're an idiot. You're useless and fat and stupid and worthless," your brain finds it very hard to remember that only one person said that. Only 1. Out of all the people you know, out of 7.7 billion humans on earth, it was just 1. But it feels like the truth.

I wonder if that's why the one true God calls you so many names. Let me show you all the names that God calls Christians in the New Testament. I counted them a while back, trying to note how often Christians were called weak or sinful by Jesus and the apostles and how often they were called holy and pure and beloved and chosen. I counted 682 total names in the New Testament. Guess how many were positive? 610! What?! 610. A 9 to 1 ratio. There's still some hard truth—we are still sinners—but he overwhelms us with the truth of our identity, who we are now through Jesus. Christian survivors of abuse are saints. They are not damaged. They are a delight to God. It's almost as if God knew how many names we would be called. So he put on every page of the Bible the reality of what the life and death and resurrection of Jesus did for us.

If you're not a Christian today, this is what Jesus is offering you. Right now. Let the Holy Spirit lead you to Jesus, call out to Jesus, trust in Jesus, and you will be saved from the old labels and so much more. You will get a new name. Lots of new names, actually. Loved, Saved, Treasured, Cherished, Child of God.

At one of Jesus' first-ever sermons, he said that this was his mission: **"The Spirit of the Lord is on me, because he has anointed me to proclaim good news to the poor. He has sent me *to proclaim freedom for the prisoners* and recovery of sight for the blind, to *set the oppressed free*"** (Luke 4:18). Jesus came with good news. His blood would cleanse us from everything embarrassing and unclean. And his words would set the oppressed, the mistreated, the abused free.

I know this might be hard to believe, so I want to offer you a clear next step. After consulting with some counselors and abuse experts, I've put together a short list of places for you to turn. These are websites, books, and organizations that can help you figure this out. Abuse lives on lies, and these places can help you hear the truth, to hear, again and again, that God loves the abused. You can find this resource list on page 101 of this book.

But there's one last thing I want you to know—*God was abused.* Did you know that? When you think of Jesus, do you think of an abuse victim? He was. The great Old Testament prophecy said, **"He was oppressed and afflicted"** (Isaiah 53:7). Jesus was struck, slapped, and stripped of his clothing. He was stricken, smitten, and afflicted. He was assaulted, mocked, and ridiculed in his pain. He ended up all alone with the men who used force to control him, to put him on a cross.

That doesn't just mean that Jesus died for you; it also means that God gets it. God gets what you're going through. He knows what it's like. When you pray to him, he nods, because he knows. Every time you see a cross, you see the proof. And just like Jesus' story didn't end in abuse, yours won't either. Easter came after Good Friday, and one day, I pray soon, Jesus will put an end to the hurt and wounds of your abuse.

Last year I was at a farmer's market with my wife, and I ran into her, the woman who had been hurt by her boyfriend. She looked good. She assured me she was good. She got free, and she was healing. She had come to see the truth about that guy and the better truth about God.

I hope you can heal too by putting your hope in Jesus. He is our Refuge, our Rock, our Savior. He came once to save us from our sins. And he will come again to save us from their sins.

Let's Pray About This

Dear Jesus, thank you for being the One I can always come to. There's not a single person who is too broken or who's been through too much that you can't reach them, you can't save them, and you can't overwhelm them with their identity in you. Jesus, two thousand years ago you could have stayed safe, you could have come down from heaven to give the world good advice, but you didn't. You came down and went through the worst of it so that I could have the best of it: A place in my Father's family, a God whom I pray to and he listens. A Father, who for many, is so different than the fathers we grew up with. I could call Jesus my brother, a perfectly safe brother. I could call him the husband to the church, a husband who only gave up his own wants and desires so that we could find hope and healing.

Thank you, God, for being you. Thank you that I can be a member of a church where I don't have to have it all together. I can go to church with all the mess and all the baggage and there you are, face shining and your favor beaming down upon me. Thank you, God, for the gospel. I pray in the days to come you will heal people, that people who have been traumatized will end abuse in their family trees. I pray that people who've been running to all the wrong places to escape the pain of their past would come forward in honest confession and find what this world simply can't offer: a whole new identity, solid and secure, by the blood of Jesus Christ.

God, I want to be a person who gets down into the ditch to help others who are stuck and lost. Let me be that kind of person. I ask it in Jesus' name. Amen.

Let's Think About This

1. Why do you suppose the church has been relatively silent on the topic of abuse? Based on what you read in this chapter, list at least three reasons why speaking on a taboo topic like this is necessary for God's people.

2. Think through the suffering that Jesus endured. In what specific ways can he relate to men and women who have been abused? How is Jesus' situation both our comfort in this life and our hope for the life to come?

3. Check out netgrace.org, which examines abuse from a Christian perspective. Let the articles and messages on the site open your eyes to both the reality of abuse and the answers that God provides in his Word and through his devoted people.

Abuse: What Does God Say to the Abusive?

We've learned what God says to people who have endured abuse. If you recall, abuse is a pattern of behavior that uses fear/force to maintain power/control. In a country where 1 in 4 women and 1 in 7 men will be victims of severe physical violence and many others are victimized by emotional or verbal or sexual or spiritual abuse, this topic is real and relevant. We learned that God hates abuse, God loves the abused, and God himself was abused. I hope those truths helped you heal in some small or miraculously big way. Now I want to address those who have been abusive. Since the good news of Jesus draws all kinds of sinners—the proud, the impure, the gossips, the worriers, the attention seekers, and the addicts—I assume that abusive people may show up at my church or might read this book too. And I want them to show up; I want them to read this.

There's a man who writes me often from prison. He's a guy who now knows Jesus, loves his Savior, and can't wait to finish his time. He's a man who laments his past, is working hard on his faith in the present, and longs for his future to be different. He's a worshiper of Jesus who wants to worship Jesus someday in my church.

One day, however, I looked up my pen pal online and saw his legal history. The words *assault of a minor* and *repeated* and *felony* grabbed my attention and broke my heart. Abuse of the worst kind is part of his story. So what would Jesus do if a guy like that was in the crowd and wanted to follow him? And what should I and my church do? If he's released and shows up on Sunday, should we lock the doors? warn the parents? "forgive and forget"? something else? Saying, "Everyone is welcome" and, "You belong here" is easy, but when people have patterns of behavior of hurting others, what then? In this chapter I want to address my friend, whom I believe watches *Time of Grace* regularly, and I want to speak to you the reader. Because there are four things every abusive person needs to hear from me and especially from God.

Here's the first thing I want you to hear—*Look at you.* I want you to take a long look at you. Depending on how you grew up, how your dad treated your mom, how your mom spoke to your dad, how the adults in your life treated you, you might not even know what abuse looks like. What might seem normal might only be normal because that's what you went through. So here is a list of questions to help you look at you:

- Do you have a pattern of getting angry when your partner or children don't do what you want?

- Do you express that anger by name-calling, threatening looks, physical threats, or physical acts like breaking things, hitting pets, grabbing wrists, blocking her from leaving, or pushing him around?

- Do you blame those moments on alcohol, drugs, or someone else's behavior—you were just drunk or high or having a stressful day; you wouldn't have done it if they wouldn't have done that?

- Do you force your partner to spend time with you and forbid them from spending time with friends and family?

- Do you get jealous or nervous when they do?

- Do you check their texts, read their personal emails, or control the finances so they have nothing unless you allow it?

- Do you force them to be intimate with you?

- Do you ever use the Bible to get what you want, telling him he has to forgive you no matter how much you belittle him and she has to submit to you because you are the head of the household? Do you believe that *submit* means they have to do what you say? That *forgive* means they have to forget?

- Have you ever threatened to hurt yourself just so they would stay?

- Are the people in your life afraid to contradict you? Do they cringe when you're angry? Do they change their plans just to appease you and avoid your anger?

If that's a pattern of your behavior, that's abuse.

And—look—God hates that. David, who was himself threatened and abused by King Saul, wrote, **"The LORD examines the righteous, but the wicked, those who love violence, he hates with a passion"** (Psalm 11:5). The biggest issue with your anger isn't that it might get you in legal trouble or end your relationship or make your kids hate you when they grow up (as one abuse victim told me). The biggest issue is that it makes God hate you. No one who continues on this path, living in this sin, hurting people God loves, will end up good with God. So before you have to stand before our Father holding a history of hurting his children, look at you. Repent. Confess. Humble yourself. Give up the control, the image, the facade, and get help.

That's the first thing I'd say to you. Here's the next thing— *Look at him*. Look at Jesus. Even if every one of those questions slapped you in the conscience and made you wish you weren't reading this, know this—Jesus is not done with you yet. If you're still alive and breathing, praise the Lord, because Jesus is waiting. Jesus is willing. If you give up control, if you repent, he is willing to call you his friend. Here's some proof. **"These are the**

names of the twelve apostles: first, Simon (who is called Peter) and his brother Andrew; James son of Zebedee, and his brother John; Philip and Bartholomew; Thomas and Matthew the tax collector; James son of Alphaeus, and Thaddaeus; Simon the Zealot and Judas Iscariot, who betrayed him" (Matthew 10:2-4). Did you catch it? Simon the Zealot. A zealot, in Jesus' day, was a violent man. The zealots hated that the Romans had control, so they used fear and force to take it back. Abusers wouldn't be totally accurate, but they had a past with violence, with victims. Yet Jesus invited a guy like that to follow a God like him.

And he wasn't the last. The apostle Paul, the guy who wrote half the New Testament, said this about himself: **"Even though I was once a blasphemer and a persecutor and a violent man, I was shown mercy because I acted in ignorance and unbelief. The grace of our Lord was poured out on me abundantly, along with the faith and love that are in Christ Jesus"** (1 Timothy 1:13,14). Paul was violent. People feared Paul's anger and cringed when he showed up at their homes, but he was called by Jesus. He confessed his sins, was baptized, and was immersed by grace and love.

Simon the Zealot and Paul the apostle were forgiven and given salvation, and you can be forgiven too because Jesus forgave even abusers. Remember our Savior hanging on a cross. After being abused, Jesus cried out, **"Father, forgive them"** (Luke 23:34). He still says that. For you. When Jesus hung on a cross, suffering for sins, he suffered for us all. And *all* includes YOU. Abuse is ugly, but Jesus took that ugliness to the cross. When you look to Jesus, God stops hating you and starts calling you his own dear child. Look at him. Look at Jesus. There will still be consequences, but when you look at Jesus, there is no condemnation (Romans 8:1). So look at him.

Third, I want you to *look at them*. Look at the people God

has placed in your community who can help you. Now that you know how much God hates abusers and how far Jesus went to forgive abusers, what will you do? How will you change? Here's how—look at them. It's very possible that the abuse didn't start with you, that you learned to yell and scream and control from your father or your mother or your mom's boyfriend. Sometimes there are generational sins that families get stuck in, ways they pass on to their children's children. Maybe that's why the abuse started. Maybe you don't know what healthy looks like. So look at them. Look at the professionals whom God has blessed with the wisdom to help you escape the cycle. It's not the job of your significant other or your kids to fix this. I know you'd rather keep this in-house, keep this quiet, hold on to your reputation, but you can't. There is hope, but you need help from the outside. The list on page 101 of this book is filled with resources for you to get help. You might be the first generation in your family in a long time to break the cycle, to break free from the chain. Take a next step. Call an abuse specialist. Go to anger management.

And now, fourth and finally, *look at me.* I'm happy that you're reading this. I'm not just saying that. I've prayed for you to read this. I've begged God that you would keep reading, so thank you. Angels rejoice when sinners repent, and I plan to join them at their party. So let me say this as clearly as I can— you are welcome at my church, at Time of Grace, and every Christian church that loves Jesus and cares about people. Even with a past, you are welcome. Even with a legal record, you are welcome. We have no plans to pick and choose which kinds of sinners can come and watch. Churches aren't country clubs with a minimum morality requirement. They're churches, and sinners are welcome. In Jesus' day, the worst people in town were tax collectors and prostitutes, but Jesus called them to repent and follow him. In our day, the categories are different, but the call is the same—sinners can be forgiven, can be changed, as they repent and follow Jesus. That is why, despite all my sins, I am welcome. That's why you are welcome.

AND—look at me: As I welcome you with open arms, I also welcome you with wisdom and with boundaries that bless you and the others in my congregation. In other words, depending on your story, things might be a bit different for you as part of a church community. We don't let the guy with a gambling addiction be the church treasurer. That's wisdom. We don't tempt alcoholics by having them buy the wine for Lord's Supper. That's wisdom. And we don't let abusive people alone in situations where abuse can happen. So, yes, we require background checks for our children's ministry. Yes, we will communicate with parole officers and craft a personal plan that meets if not exceeds the requirements of the law. Yes, I realize you might not like that. No, I'm not going to change my mind about that, and neither will many church leaders. Because we care about you. And we care about others.

I imagine that's hard to hear. If you have a history of craving power and control, those rules take all of it away from you. That's actually the point. If sinfully getting control was your issue, then taking away control is your solution. I want you to get better. And this is the path to better. Please don't run. Please don't push back. Humble yourself, and God will exalt you.

Because both modern abuse experts and Jesus' apostles agree—when you are truly sorry, you are willing to show it. The apostle Paul wrote, **"See what this godly sorrow has produced in you: what earnestness, what eagerness to clear yourselves, what indignation, what alarm, what longing, what concern, what readiness to see justice done"** (2 Corinthians 7:11). I hope you are the same. I hope God is producing in you a deep desire to clear yourself, to prove that you've changed, to do whatever you can to show that things are different now, that you're giving up control.

It makes me think of a man I met a few years back. I met him in jail through a member of our church, and when he got out, he wondered if he would be welcome at the church. Our church leaders discussed it for a long time, working with his parole officer and pouring over the issue in prayer, thinking of this precious soul craving a Christian community and thinking of our own children and the children at the church we loved. Eventually, we said we'd love to have him, but there would be boundaries, restrictions, and other people who would need to know. And this guy—to his immense credit—said, "The more people who know, the better. The more accountable I will be."

He humbled himself, gave up the power and the control, submitted himself to the boundaries we created, and God exalted him. God lifted him up and gave him a church home. Even better, God brought him to a place where he would hear, week after week, something that the world would never tell him—that he was forgiven, saved, and loved through Jesus. He was at my church last Sunday.

The same can happen to you. I pray that it does.

Let's Pray About This

Father in heaven, thank you for forgiving things that this world doesn't. There are certain sins that some of us have committed that if our neighbors knew, they wouldn't give us a second chance. And, God, you didn't give us a second chance; you gave us your one and only Son. Thank you for your grace, which is truly unconditional love. Thank you that I am saved, not by the works that I do or the life that I live but as a free gift at the cross of Jesus Christ.

I pray, heavenly Father, for wisdom for church leaders. I pray for every pastor and ministry leader that they would not do the easy thing and give abusers an automatic no or an automatic yes, but they would do the hard work of welcoming them with love. I pray that through the message of the gospel more and more people can be saved.

I especially pray, heavenly Father, for those in prison who write to Pastor Mike. Only you can change their hearts. Humble them and help them find something way greater than power and control in the fact that they are your children through faith in Jesus Christ. Produce in them gentleness, kindness, patience, self-control, and love; that the statistics can start to change in some small way.

Once again, Father, for those who are carrying the wounds of abuse, I pray that this book would give them more hope to know that they can continue to find healing. I pray that in some small or miraculously big way you would change people through it. I ask it all in Jesus' name. Amen.

Let's Think About This

1. What happens when the church is too quick to "forgive and forget" the sin of abuse? What happens when the church has no place for repentant abusers among its members? What would you write about abusers if you were tasked with creating the church policy on addressing abuse?

2. Agree/Disagree: If Jesus was known for loving prostitutes, tax collectors, and the worst sinners of his day, faithful Christians should be known for loving the abusive, registered sex offenders, and the worst sinners of our day.

26

3. Evaluate: God wants our churches to tell the abusive to repent/ change, to offer them the free gift of God's grace, and to have unwavering boundaries as a necessary consequence of their past behavior.

Abuse: What Does God Say to the Church?

What should you do when you learn about abuse? In the last two chapters, I've been talking about abuse, what God says to the abused and what God says to the abusive. Remember that abuse is a pattern of behavior that uses fear/force to maintain power/control. But what should you do when you're not the victim or the victimizer but rather the friend, the family member, the fellow Christian who learns about abuse?

Many years ago, I had to wrestle with that question. A woman came into my office with her children and confessed to me that they did not have a happy home life, that her husband was hurting her and the kids—physically and verbally and emotionally. What was more, I knew the guy; I was his pastor too, which meant that within days I would sit with him in the same room and address the same issue. What would I say to the kids, to her, to him? What would I do?

What would you do? Given the widespread numbers of abuse, you and I know and love and worship next to people who have been impacted by abuse. In some way, the truth about that abuse will reach your ears. Your friend shares some concerning details of the fight she had with her boyfriend. While she says, "It was my fault," the bruise on her wrist tells a different story. Your nephew jokes about your brother's parenting in a way that feels . . . off. Your roommate starts dating a girl who belittles him in public and checks his phone in private, the girl he constantly worries he might make angry. Someone at your Bible study group tells the story of an emotionally abusive mother. Or someone confesses that they have been a verbally abusive father. In those moments, what should you and I, as God's people, do?

There is one passage of the Bible that answers that question. It's a tough passage to translate from the original Hebrew, but it gives clear guidance on how to love both the abused and the abusive.

Check out Isaiah 1:17: **"Learn to do right; seek justice. Defend the oppressed."** God wants us to learn to do the right thing, to seek justice (that means protecting the innocent and punishing the guilty), and to defend the oppressed. My dictionary says that *oppressed* means "ill-treated, tyrannized, or . . . abused." God wants us to defend the abused.

The word *defend* makes me picture an ancient city, like Jerusalem, with its towering walls and strong gates, a place built to keep dangerous people outside and to keep people safe inside. So picture yourself standing on top of the wall with people you love huddled inside, and an abusive person comes riding up toward the city. How do you protect your loved ones? How do you defend the oppressed? Two strategies come to mind.

First, you defend the oppressed with *TRUTH*. Abuse can only exist when lies get the last word, so when you immerse yourself in truth, in what God sees, in what God says, you defend the oppressed. For example, an abuser lies to his victim and says, "This is your fault," even though it isn't. "This isn't abuse," even though it is. "You made me do that," even though he freely chose to do it. But truth turns up the lights, takes off the makeup, and shows things for what they really are.

More truth leads to less abuse. Which is why I want to direct you again to the resource list at the back of this book to help you know the truth. You'll find websites, sermons, books, and qualified counselors who can help, who want to help. There are resources listed that describe what abuse is, how abuse survives, and how you can avoid or survive abuse. The book *Rid of My Disgrace* is the most honest, professional, grace-centered book on sexual abuse that I have ever read. It opened my eyes to see what abuse can look like in a relationship and how Jesus heals and cleanses and is with people who have endured abuse. Whatever resources you choose, choose truth, because that's how you defend the oppressed.

Second, defend the oppressed with *GRACE*. With undeserved, persistent, enduring love. I once knew a woman who had been badly abused by her significant other (men are sometimes abused by women too, so forgive my one-sided stories here). The details of what she had suffered were heartbreaking and hard to hear . . . and yet, despite calling the cops, she went back to him. And I realized how complicated this all is. There are factors, childhood wounds, generational sins, and decades-long habits that keep us caught up in abuse.

That's why grace is so essential—your willingness to wait, to be there, to love. As your friend fights to believe it really isn't his fault, grace waits. As your sister moves out and then moves back in with him, grace prays. As your daughter goes back to the guy you want to run over with your truck, grace is there when she calls. Abuse is more complicated than you think. You don't just say, "That's bad! Run away!" and it works the first time. Grace is being ready whenever they're ready, like the father of the prodigal son who waited until his boy came home.

And while you wait, grace gives the gospel. If the abused is a Christian, you can say, "You are a child of God. You are so precious to our Father. He loves you. He delights in you. He doesn't think you're worthless or stupid or useless. He smiles when he thinks of you."

If the abused isn't a Christian, you can say, "God wants something better for you. He is a Father who doesn't hurt his children. Jesus is a husband who doesn't use the 'head of the household' to get his way but to love his bride. Jesus understands what you are going through. He wants you to have the hope of a place where there is no more crying or tears or abuse." Give the gospel, and you give the best grace of all, the grace of our Lord Jesus Christ.

God said to defend the oppressed. Defend them with grace. Defend them with truth. But what about the oppressor? What do you say to the abusive? Well, this same passage might say something about that too. Isaiah 1:17 says, **"Learn to do right. Seek justice. Defend the oppressed,"** but I bet your Bible, like mine, has a little footnote, a little letter to click on in your digital Bible, a note that says: "Or—here's another valid translation—correct the oppressor." I know that's kind of confusing, but sometimes a sentence can be understood in two ways. This might be saying that we should learn to correct the oppressor. Confront the abuser.

Remember the mom with the kids who told me about her abusive home life? Well, I got to confront the abuser. I'll never forget that conversation because of how much he cried and how much I didn't. He told me, swore to me, wept to me that he never did any of it. But I didn't believe him. God, forgive me if I was wrong, but I was 99 percent sure he was trying to manipulate me to maintain power and control. So I said—this is the only time I've ever said this in counseling—"I don't believe you. No, you are lying to me." I straight-faced him because I felt that defending the oppressed meant correcting the oppressor.

Warning—Abusive people are, as one expert emailed me, "tough nuts to crack." When lies have been your language for so long, the truth seems strange. When you're used to doing anything to come out with control, being asked to confess and submit and be humble is the hardest thing in the world. Especially in churches that value the beauty of a husband's call to lead like Jesus or the power of limitless forgiveness, abusers can take truth to places that God never intended, to redefine words in ways to which Jesus would have objected. Helping an abuser become a safe person who is welcome inside the walls is not for the faint of heart. So what do you do? You correct the oppressor with *TRUTH*.

Here's the truth: "Abuse is your fault. Abuse is your choice. Yours. Even if he . . . even if she . . . you made the choice to do that, to say that. Okay, you were drunk, but you made the choice to drink. I know you were stressed, but not every stressed person does that. This is on you. This is your issue. God isn't into excuses, so stop making them. Adam tried to blame Eve, but God wasn't hearing it. Own it. Confess it. Because if you hurt one of God's kids, our Father is not going to be happy with you. That power you feel when you rule under your roof—that power will cost you paradise.

"And the truth is that you need help. You need professional counseling. You can't turn off your anger and jealousy and craving for control like a light switch. You need someone or a group of people who can help you. I'll help you. I'll help you find a counselor, meet with the pastor, keep you accountable. But you need help. It's time to humble yourself. Time to give up power. Time to give up control. I'm not running away from you, but I am telling you to leave behind your lies." That's the truth.

But an abuser needs more than truth. They also need *GRACE*. And some of my church members told me I needed to say that. Recently, 159 members of my church completed a survey to help me prepare for this book. One of the themes that came up a lot was not letting the church decide, because of the hurt and messiness, that some people aren't allowed to come. Not letting the church decide that abusers can't come, no matter how sorry they are or how hard they are trying to change. Instead, the church is to offer grace to everyone. Look at what God says next.

The very next verse in Isaiah chapter 1, after exposing the ugliness of oppression and sin, says, **"Though your sins are like scarlet, they shall be as white as snow; though they are red as crimson, they shall be like wool"** (verse 18). Yes, abuse is a sin that stains us in ways we can't wash out. But God can. Jesus was abused on a cross so that even abusers could be saved, so that you could come to him with all of the consequences and end up with no condemnation, so that God himself could look at you and see someone who brings him joy, someone who has been rescued by Jesus.

Grace and truth. For the abused. For the abusive. Truth to see sin as it really is, to see ourselves as we really are. Grace to heal our wounds, to ease our consciences, to get us back to God. It might be messy, it might take time, but grace and truth are how we defend and correct, how we help, and how we love.

In those 159 surveys, there was one comment that really grabbed my attention. It's a reminder of what is at stake as I write this book and talk about abuse. One person who took the survey admitted that they had been abused and then added, "If you can save just one person from the situation they are in, you have done a wonderful thing." I hope that grace and truth, for the abused and the abusive, from me and through you in the days to come, saves many more than one. Because in God's eyes, that would truly be a wonderful thing.

Let's Pray About This

Gracious Lord, please give me wisdom. You've said in your Word that if we lack wisdom, if we just don't know what to do in a situation, we could ask you in faith and you would give it. I thank you for the wisdom you've already given.

But, God, humbly, I want to ask you for more.

Let these words from Isaiah be the seed in my heart that you water and grow so that I can become the kind of person who corrects and protects, a person who addresses and defends. Father, you know the statistics. In fact, you know better than the statistics. Our world, our culture, needs help. Help me be a helper who serves in your name.

Thank you, Jesus, for your love, for your presence, for sending your Spirit, and for the power that I have in you to do the right thing at the right time that your people, your church, and this world could be blessed. I pray all these things with faith in you, Jesus. Amen.

Let's Think About This

1. Have you ever tried to help someone who has been abused? If so, what did you do that worked? Having read this chapter, is there anything you wish you would have done differently?

2. Have you ever tried to help someone who has been abusive?
    If so, what did you do that worked? Having read this chapter,
    is there anything you wish you would have done differently?

3. Meditate on Isaiah 1:17-20. Find two to three other truths in this section that help prepare you to help the people whom God will place in your path in the days to come.

Devotions
&
Further Study

Part 1: God's Word for the Abused

The Lord is close to the brokenhearted
and saves those who are crushed in spirit.

Psalm 34:18

God Is Close to the Abused

While abuse is not a comfortable topic to talk about, we need to. If the Centers for Disease Control and Prevention's statistics are correct, 59,000 people who watch *Time of Grace* on TV each week have suffered some type of abuse in their lives. By "abuse" I mean, as the National Domestic Violence Hotline defines it, a pattern of behavior that uses fear or force to maintain power and control.

Maybe that description hits home. Your dad was aggressive in his physical discipline. Your mom degraded you with her words. Your boyfriend isolated you from your friends, pushed until he got his way, or gave you an allowance as a grown woman. Your wife twisted Scripture ("You have to forgive me!") and swore she would hurt herself if you talked to the pastor. Your husband abused the Word ("You have to submit to me!") and threatened to take the kids if you didn't do exactly what he wanted.

There are many things that God says in response to the tragedy of abuse, but here is the place we must start: **"The Lord is close to the brokenhearted and saves those who are crushed in spirit"** (Psalm 34:18). When fear or force breaks our hearts and crushes our spirits, God is near. He is close to us, grieving the sins committed against us and promising to heal our wounds.

Given the statistics and our experiences, we pray that Jesus would come and save us soon. But until that day arrives, may you always remember that the Lord is close. God is here.

1. Abuse includes way more than his raised fist and her black eye. List at least five examples of behavior that uses fear or force to maintain power and control.

2. How does God's presence provide specific comfort to those who believe they are "broken" or unworthy of love?

3. Pray for God's peace for the woman who sent the following message. Think through and write down what you would say if you were in my shoes: "Your sermon was unlike anything I have heard before, and it hit me. . . . The way I was taught about God was extremely law driven and was used to make me do what my dad wanted me to do out of fear. I am interested in knowing the God you have, but how can that God want me to believe in him when I am this type of person? I have openly said I hate God and even said he isn't real because if he was, he would have saved me from some of the things that happened. I have been told by family members that I am damaged goods. Is that how your God would see me?"

Abuse Is Not Your Fault

As I prepared a series of messages on the topic of abuse, I sent my first drafts to a woman I knew who specialized in domestic violence, hoping to speak more accurately and helpfully to those who had suffered trauma in their lives.

Her feedback was priceless. In particular, I remember her saying that one of the most important things for victims to hear is, "It's not your fault." Abusive people have a way of finger-pointing and blame shifting, convincing us that if only we hadn't ________, they wouldn't have hurt us. It's sick, but it's common. And it's a key way that abuse continues for months or years on end.

So let me be as clear as my colleague encouraged me to be—*It's not your fault.* Your sin is your fault, but their sin is not your fault. It's their fault. Read that last sentence again. Say it out loud until you believe it in your heart. It's not your fault.

When Jesus taught, **"If anyone causes one of these little ones—those who believe in me—to stumble,"** he didn't go on to blame the little children for the grown-ups' sins (Matthew 18:6). Why not? Because the sin wasn't their fault.

Healing from abuse is hard enough. So please believe the voice of the One who loves you. Abuse is not your fault.

1. Why do victims of abuse so often blame themselves instead
   of their abusers? How might that self-blame be an enslaving
   lie from the father of lies himself (John 8:44)?

2. Read the following message from a sister in Christ, and list at least two connections to the previous devotion: "Even today I struggle with thinking that I could have done something differently to keep him from acting like that—maybe he just didn't realize what he was doing, maybe I should have realized and said something sooner, maybe he was just trying to help. . . . What's happening to the abused person might be extremely subtle. The person might be totally convinced that there's nothing wrong or that they're the problem and just need to try harder to fix it."

3. Find a mirror, look yourself in the eye, and repeat these words: *The abuse was not my fault.* Write those words here:

God Loves the Abused

A few years back, a pastor told me about the funny way our minds do math. He had just read a study that said when one person says something to you ten times and ten people say something to you one time, our brains feel about the same. In other words, 1x10 = 1+1+1+1+1+1+1+1+1+1. So if your mom or your boyfriend constantly says, "You're so dumb. You're an idiot. You're useless and fat and stupid and worthless," your brain finds it very hard to remember that only one person said that. Only one. But it feels like the truth.

I wonder if that's why the one true God calls you so many names. Throughout the New Testament, there are over 680 names that God calls those who believe in Jesus. Guess how many are positive, names like Holy or Beloved or Blameless or Pure? Not 1 or 2 or 10, but 610! Despite all of our struggles and sins, God himself has 610 names to lift us up and give us hope.

If you are one of the many people who carry the wounds of abuse, turn your ear today toward Jesus. Through his death and resurrection, he wants to overwhelm your mind with love and set you free. As Jesus himself said, **"[God] has sent me to proclaim freedom for the prisoners . . . to set the oppressed free"** (Luke 4:18).

1. Meditate on each of the names that God calls you in 1 Peter 2:9: **"But you are a chosen people, a royal priesthood, a holy nation, God's special possession."** What do these names mean to you?

2. Is there any one person from your past (or present) who sinfully degraded you by name-calling? If so, remind your wounded heart that God himself, the source of truth, disagrees. Write here again what God says about you.

3. Write your favorite name that God calls you in his Word in this space. Stare at it for an entire minute. Let the truth of who you are in Jesus bring comfort to your soul.

4. Rejoice with and react to the following email: "I wanted to reach out and thank you for yesterday's message and series about abuse. As a kid who grew up in a violent home, this issue is near and dear to my heart. Throughout the years of attending service, I have never once heard this critical topic addressed. . . . Your ongoing grace with the subject is going to help a lot of other suffering people. I just know it!"

God Hates Abuse

A man came to my office and confessed to me that he had been abusive with his girlfriend. After expressing my grave concern for his behavior, I told the man what I would tell any seemingly repentant sinner—Jesus forgives you. Although there would be consequences for his actions, Jesus had taken away his eternal condemnation. I even texted him a Bible passage so the guilt wouldn't overwhelm him. (FYI—I also consulted law enforcement to see what I could do to keep this woman safe from future abuse.)

A while later, however, his girlfriend stopped by my office and told me what had happened next. The man had taken my text, shoved it in her face, and boasted, "See! Even the pastor is on my side!" My heart slumped as she repeated his words, and I came to hate abuse more than I ever had in my life.

"Those who love violence, [the Lord] **hates with a passion"** (Psalm 11:5). That passage is a terrifying reminder that God hates not just abuse but abusers themselves. If you have endured abuse, let these stark words remind you that God is on your side, close to the brokenhearted and passionate about justice. As the psalm goes on to say, **"**[The Lord] **loves justice; the upright will see his face"** (verse 7).

1. One woman emailed me to say, "I have come to realize that I am very angry with God." How could the words of Psalm 11 help to save this woman's relationship with our Father?

2. Evaluate: The word *hates* in Psalm 11:5 contains healing power for those who have been abused.

3. If you carry the traumatic memories of abuse, tell yourself or write it here, "God hated that." Be as specific as you can. "God hated it when my dad called me worthless." "God hated it when my boyfriend punched the wall."

4. A colleague in ministry with great experience in this area messaged, "Abuse happens to men and women. . . . I try to avoid making men the guilty ones and women the abused ones. Men already find it hard to speak up, I believe in part because women are always portrayed as the victim." How could you learn from her wisdom as you seek to help as many people as possible?

God Gets Your Abuse

Have you ever been going through something in life and had a conversation with someone who truly understood what you were going through? Maybe you were dealing with daily anxiety or divorce court or a family member who was walking away from church, but God gave you a person who had walked in your shoes and could relate to your pain. Isn't there something powerful about such moments? Even if your situation doesn't change, there's something about knowing that other people understand.

Maybe that's why Jesus was abused. An old prophecy about his suffering predicted, **"He was oppressed and afflicted"** (Isaiah 53:7), which Jesus felt in the soldiers' fists, their verbal taunts, and the crown of thorns they pressed onto his head. Our Savior was physically, verbally, and emotionally shamed behind closed doors and on a hill outside of Jerusalem for everyone to see.

Jesus' experience on earth means that he gets what it's like to be abused. When you call out to him in your prayers, Jesus doesn't wrinkle his forehead in confusion, unable to relate to your situation. Instead, his head nods slowly and his eyes brim with compassion. He knows what that's like. He has felt that pain. He has carried those wounds.

One day, Jesus will come back and end abuse once and for all. Until that day comes, however, he walks by our sides and listens to our prayers as the Son of God who gets it. Jesus gets you.

1. Take a few minutes to consider the abuse that Jesus endured in the last 24 hours of his life (Matthew 26:47-75; 27:11-56; Mark 14:43-72; 15:1-41; Luke 22:47-71; 23:1-49; John 18:1-40; 19:1-37). Who abused him? How was he abused? How does his passion make him a Savior who truly understands you?

2. A member of my church wrote, "It has been very soul soothing to see the church tackle tough issues like abuse. I have been on a long journey with God on this very issue for about four years now and have been searching for help in the church." Why do you suppose that just talking about this issue was "soul soothing" for this member of God's family?

3. The word *compassion* is a compound word that literally means "to suffer (passion) with (com)." How does knowing we have a God of immense compassion help us when our memories pull us back into past trauma?

Part 2: God's Word for the Abusive

Even though I was once a blasphemer and a persecutor and a violent man, I was shown mercy because I acted in ignorance and unbelief. The grace of our Lord was poured out on me abundantly, along with the faith and love that are in Christ Jesus.

1 Timothy 1:13,14

God Exalts the Humble

Around 2014, I met a man who had committed a felony against a minor. When the man was released from jail, he wondered if he would be welcome as a part of our church family. Our church leaders discussed it for a long time, working with his parole officer and pouring over the issue in prayer, thinking of this precious soul craving a Christian community and thinking of our own children at the church we loved. Eventually, we said we'd love to have him, but there would be boundaries, restrictions, and other people who would need to know.

This guy—to his immense credit—said, "The more people who know, the better. I will stand in front of church and tell everyone if that's what you want. It will only make me more accountable." So that's what we did. And I am ecstatic to tell you that years later, this brother in Christ is still an active member of our church family, hearing about God's unending grace Sunday after Sunday in our midst.

Jesus once promised, **"Those who humble themselves will be exalted"** (Luke 18:14). You might have a complicated story or sins serious enough to come with legal consequences. But by the blood of Christ, that doesn't have to stop you from being a child of God, equal in status to every other Christian. Cry out in humility to Jesus, and you will be exalted.

1. Agree/Disagree: Abusers should be welcomed into Christian churches.

2. What boundaries, restrictions, and people would a church need to consider as it seeks to make its community a safe, gracious, and healing environment for all who attend?

3. Pray today for someone you know who has abused others that God would humble their proud heart and lead them to true repentance. If that person is you, pray for the Holy Spirit to help you believe that future exaltation comes through present humility. Write your prayer here.

Look at You

Depending on how you grew up, how your dad treated your mom, how your mom spoke to your dad, or how the adults in your life treated you, you might not know what abuse looks like.

Here are some glimpses of what abuse is: Do you have a pattern of getting angry when your partner or children don't do what you want? Do you express anger by name-calling, threatening looks, physical threats, or physical acts like breaking things or hurting pets? Do you blame those outbursts on alcohol, drugs, or someone else? Do you ever use the Bible to get what you want, telling him he has to forgive you no matter how much you belittle him and she has to submit because you are the head of the household? If that happens often, that's abuse. (And if you don't want others to read these words, it's likely you are abusive.)

I need you to know how much God hates abuse. **"Those who love violence,** [the Lord] **hates with a passion"** (Psalm 11:5). The biggest issue with your behavior isn't that it might get you in legal trouble or cost you control at home. The biggest issue is that it makes God hate you. No one who continues living in this sin, hurting people God loves, will end up loved by God. So before you have to stand before our Father holding a history of hurting his children, look at you.

And before the guilt of your sin overwhelms you, please run to Jesus. There is hope in his name for every sinner, even for you.

1. Did any of the examples in this devotion hit close to home?
   Which one do you need to confess to God today? Which one
   might be the most tempting for you in the days to come?

2. Evaluate: Reading Psalm 11:5 in church could cause some people to leave and never come back.

3. React to the following message from a sister in the faith: "I don't know if you realize how grateful abuse victims are finally to have someone speak out when you suspect abuse. I don't know how much impact it has on the abusers, but the abused need to know that other people see it, know they are hurting, need someone they can confide in, and there is a shoulder they can cry on."

Look at Him

If you've ever used fear or force to maintain control in a relationship, I want you to look at Jesus. Psalm 11 says that the Lord hates those who love violence, a blunt fact that I hope leads you to repent and cry out to God for forgiveness.

Because there's hope even for abusive people. The apostle Paul is the proof. **"Even though I was once a blasphemer and a persecutor and a violent man, I was shown mercy because I acted in ignorance and unbelief. The grace of our Lord was poured out on me abundantly, along with the faith and love that are in Christ Jesus"** (1 Timothy 1:13,14). Paul was, by his own admission, a violent man, yet when God opened his eyes to the depth of his sin, Paul found mercy, grace, and love through Jesus.

You can be saved too, because Jesus forgave abusers. After being slapped and spit on, mocked and nailed to a cross, Jesus cried out, **"Father, forgive them"** (Luke 23:34). He still says that, and every sinner who is truly sorry receives that. Abuse is ugly, but Jesus took that ugliness to the cross. When you look to Jesus, when you change your mind about who is in control, God stops hating you and starts calling you his own dear child. So look at Jesus. With me, with us, look at Jesus. There will still be consequences, but when you look at Jesus, there is no condemnation (Romans 8:1).

1. Meditate on each of the following words from this devotion: *mercy, grace, abundantly, faith, love, Christ Jesus.* Which brings you the most comfort? Why?

2. One man sheepishly admitted, "This was about me." How do
   you suppose that man would feel if he read Paul's words from
   1 Timothy 1:13,14?

3. Find (or purchase) a piece of Christian art that depicts the
   cross of Jesus Christ. Display it in a prominent place in your
   room so that you can "look at him" more than ever before.

Look at Me

If I knew that one hundred abusive people showed up at our church on a Sunday, I would say, "Look at me. I'm happy you're here. This is a Christian church where sinners are welcome. In Jesus' day, the worst people in town were tax collectors and prostitutes, but Jesus called them to follow him. We want to be like Jesus, so you are welcome to follow Jesus here too."

And then, with all the compassion in my heart, I would continue: "And we welcome you with wisdom. We don't let the gambling addict be the church treasurer. We don't tempt alcoholics by having them buy the wine for Lord's Supper. And we don't let abusive people alone in situations where abuse can happen. So, yes, we require background checks for our children's ministry. Yes, we will communicate with parole officers and craft a personal plan that meets and, perhaps, exceeds the requirements of the law. Because we care about you and about everyone else."

I'm not sure how that message would be received, but I know what the Bible says about those who are truly repentant: **"See what this godly sorrow has produced in you: what earnestness, what eagerness to clear yourselves, what indignation, what alarm, what longing, what concern, what readiness to see justice done"** (2 Corinthians 7:11). People who are truly sorry will take steps to prove it, submitting to the leadership of the church.

If you have a history of abusive behavior and want to change, go to church. Even if there are consequences for your past, a good church can help you walk with Jesus for your eternal future.

1. Evaluate: Background checks are a sign of distrust that have little place in a loving church community.

2. Do you believe that a Christian church should be the most honest and welcoming place for everyone in your community? Why or why not?

3. Study 2 Corinthians chapter 7. Based on Paul's approach to sin in the Corinthian church, how would he handle your situation in a local church today?

Look at Them

Abuse is a complicated issue that often has generational roots. As the saying goes, "Hurt people hurt people." If you were raised by a father who used the back of his hand to threaten you or a mother who degraded you daily with her words, you might have ended up in a fog about how relationships are supposed to work. The abused can easily turn into abusers.

This is why it's essential for us to look around at the people God has placed in our path who are able to help us heal. Jesus' half brother James wrote, **"Therefore confess your sins to each other and pray for each other so that you may be healed. The prayer of a righteous person is powerful and effective"** (James 5:16). There's healing power in the people of God. When you confess your sins to others and they, in turn, pray for you, you can heal wounds and change behaviors far faster than if you were on your own.

Today, I'm asking you to look at them. At your pastor, if you have one. At Christian counselors in your area who specialize in abuse. At friends who know you, love Jesus, and have healthy relationships. Yes, it will be humbling to confess your sins and your story to them. Yes, there might be consequences to the truth coming out. But it's the best step in the world to take.

If you come from a long line of hurting people, the cycle can stop. Your family tree can change. Please look at them. It's how God will help and heal us.

1. Agree/Disagree: Abusers, like alcoholics, don't really want to change.

2. Is "hurt people hurt people" an excuse for sin or an explanation of it? How might that phrase be a useful tool in the hands of a wise church family?

3. A grateful member of our church family reached out to say, "I'm sitting here watching your sermon with tears streaming down my face. Sobbing actually. Thank you so much for addressing such a prevalent problem. . . . I had pretended for so many years that it wasn't as bad as it was. I spent many days sitting in church pews just hoping someone could see how sad I was or care enough to make me talk about it . . . and tell me it was OK to leave. From the bottom of my heart . . . Thank you." How do her words encourage you to reach out for personal and professional help?

Part 3: God's Word for the Church

[The Son] came from the Father,
full of grace and truth.

John 1:14

Abusers at Church?

There's a man in prison who watches *Time of Grace* and writes me grateful, encouraging, and faith-filled letters. One day, however, I came across his legal history online, and the words *assault of a minor* and *repeated* and *felony* grabbed my attention and broke my heart. I thought about this man's potential release and the possibility that he would show up on Sunday to worship next to me and my family. As I considered the glory of his forgiveness and the reality that his sin could happen again, I agonized over the question, "What would Jesus do?"

If a man with an abusive history was in the crowd in the first century, what would Jesus do? And what should we do today? Should we lock the church doors when certain types of sinners get out of their cars? warn the parents? "forgive and forget"? Saying, "Everyone is welcome" is easy, but when everyone includes *everyone*, what then?

I want to wrestle with that question by speaking directly to people who have committed the sin of abuse. This description of Jesus will guide my words: **"[The Son] came from the Father, full of grace and truth"** (John 1:14). To do what Jesus did means to be people who are full of grace and truth, Christians who care about "the least of these" without watering down undeserved love while also holding to the highest standards of truth and healthy boundaries.

What does that mean for us? Keep reading, and you will find out God's ways to help both the abused and the abusive.

1. If you knew an abusive person was showing up for church, what would you do? What wouldn't you do?

2. Evaluate: It is both easy and convenient to be full of either grace or truth, but it is the hardest thing in the world to be full of both grace and truth.

3. A middle-aged brother in the Lord sent this message: "Thanks for being open and honest with abuse. We were glad to see the resources available. . . . We can relate well here." When talking about abuse, why is a list of resources (counselors, books, passages, etc.) so valuable?

How to Help the Abused (& Abusive)

Many years ago, a woman came into my office and confessed to me that her husband was hurting her and her kids physically and verbally. What was more, the husband was also a member of our church, which meant that within days I would sit with him in the same room and address the same issue. God was calling me to help both the abused and the abusive.

Given the widespread numbers on abuse, God will call you to do the same. Maybe your friend shares some concerning details of the fight she had with her boyfriend, and the bruise on her wrist tells the rest of the story. Or your nephew jokes about your brother's parenting in a way that feels . . . off. Or your roommate starts dating a girl who belittles him in public and checks his phone in private. He worries constantly that he might make her angry. In those moments, when abuse is right in front of us, what should God's people do?

In the devotions to come, I want to explore that question as we meditate on a single verse from Isaiah: **"Learn to do right; seek justice. Defend the oppressed"** (Isaiah 1:17). Some of God's greatest work is using his forgiven children to help and heal the hurting. I pray these words enable us to do just that.

Perhaps today, when this devotion is done, you could pray for wisdom and compassion to do what is right in a world filled with the wrongs of abuse.

1. Did anyone come to mind when you read this devotion? Have you noticed any red flags in the relationships of people whom you love?

2. Imagine attending a small group where one person confesses the abuse they have suffered while another person confesses the abuse they have committed. How would you react if your goal was to do what is right toward everyone in the room?

3. A fellow Christian emailed this encouragement: "Although I have found great value and guidance from pastors on the internet, I believe we Christians need to be connected to a local body of believers and get the support we need as humans from our local church families. I give Pastor a big shout-out for taking the time to sit with me and answer hard biblical questions I had about abuse." What blessings does God love to give us when we have a face-to-face connection with other Christians in a local church?

4. Write a prayer for wisdom and compassion to do what is right. The world needs your God-inspired good work.

Help the Abused With Truth

If you know someone who's been abused, you need to read and heed Isaiah's words: **"Learn to do right; seek justice. Defend the oppressed"** (Isaiah 1:17). The word *defend* makes me picture an ancient city with towering walls and strong gates, a place built to keep dangerous people out and to keep people safe inside. So picture yourself standing on top of the wall with people you love huddled inside as an abusive person comes riding up toward the city? How do you protect your loved ones?

With truth. Abuse can only exist when lies get the last word, so when we immerse ourselves in truth, in what God sees, in what God says, we defend the oppressed. For example, an abuser lies to his victim and says, "This is your fault," even though it isn't. "This isn't abuse," even though it is. "You made me do that," even though he/she freely chose to do it. But truth turns up the lights, takes off the makeup, and shows things for what they really are.

More truth leads to less abuse. Therefore, Isaiah is encouraging us to be people whose lips speak the truth that's overflowing out of our hearts. No, the process will not be easy (abusers are good at lying, and the abused are accustomed to being lied to). But, yes, the process will be godly. Because our God loves to defend the oppressed.

So speak up and speak the truth. Then do it again tomorrow. And the next day. Until the Day when Truth himself returns.

1. List three truths that the abused often forget. Why would those things seem so apparent to you but not so apparent to them? Is there a story or analogy that you could use to help communicate that truth effectively to them?

2. What can we learn from the heartbreaking words of this abuse victim? How might her words affect which truths we share from God's Word? "That is another horrible result of the abuse, living with the feeling of hating your father. We know we are supposed to forgive, but when the abuse runs for so long and cuts so deep, it's not easy to do."

3. Take ten minutes this week to educate yourself on abuse. A simple internet search should lead you to many professional resources to open your eyes to the forms that abuse takes and the lies that many abused people believe.

Help the Abused With Grace

I once knew a woman who had been badly abused by her significant other and yet, despite calling the cops, went back to him. In that moment, I realized how complicated abuse is. There are factors—childhood wounds, generational sins, and decades-long habits—that keep us caught up in toxic and oppressive relationships.

The prophet Isaiah once wrote, **"Learn to do right; seek justice. Defend the oppressed"** (Isaiah 1:17). How do we do that? Not simply with truth but also with God's grace.

As your friend fights to believe the abuse really isn't his fault, grace waits. As your daughter goes back to the guy you want to run over with your truck, grace stands by. Grace is being ready whenever they're ready, like the father of the prodigal son who waited until his boy came home.

And grace gives the gospel. If the victim is a Christian, you can say, "You are a child of God. You are precious to our Father. He doesn't think you're worthless or stupid or useless. He smiles when he thinks of you." If the abused isn't a Christian, you can say, "God wants something better for you. Jesus understands what you're going through. He wants you to have the hope of a place where there is no more crying or tears or abuse." Grace defends the abused from an eternity of pain by promising them eternal life through Jesus.

Defend the oppressed with the gospel, giving them Jesus, the best grace of all.

1. Why don't more abused people run away from their abusers?
    List at least five logical reasons to increase your compassion
    for those in such situations.

2. Agree/Disagree: The more we preach the gospel of God's incredible love, the more likely a victim of abuse will reach out for help.

3. How would you respond to the following message from a hurting woman? "I want to not be angry, but I feel like God does not like me. . . . I want to understand why so much has happened out of my control and to feel loved. There is light in my life, but I often feel that my life's journey is pain on pain and hurt on hurt."

Help Abusers With Truth

I once accused a man of being a liar. Following a conversation with his wife and daughters, three quiet women who quietly told me about his abusive behavior, I met with the man himself. He swore to me that he was absolutely innocent. May God forgive me if I was wrong, but I was 99 percent sure he was trying to manipulate me to maintain control in his home, so I told him he was a liar and needed to repent.

In some tough-to-translate Hebrew, my Bible says, **"Defend the oppressed,"** but there's a footnote that suggests this passage might mean, **"Correct the oppressor"** (Isaiah 1:17). Whatever the right translation, that's a biblical idea. People who oppress/hurt/abuse other people need to be corrected strongly and unwaveringly.

What might that correcting sound like? Perhaps like this: "Abuse is your choice. Yours. Even if he . . . even if she . . . you made the choice to threaten your kids. Okay, you were drunk when you spewed those words, but you made the choice to drink. I know you were stressed, but not every stressed person smashes things. This is on you. And you need help. You can't turn off your anger and jealousy and craving for control like a light switch. It's time to humble yourself. Time to give up control, confess your sins, and seek professional help. That's the truth."

Will it work? Maybe, maybe not. But God calls us, for the sake of every soul involved, to correct the oppressor. Is there someone God is calling you to correct today?

1. Why must a good church be a judgmental place? In other words, why must a healthy spiritual community judge, criticize, and even condemn certain behaviors? How do your answers correct the modern infatuation with "judgment-free zones"?

92

2. What percentage of abusers will respond to God's truth? How does your answer drive you back to the supernatural work of the Spirit and God's surprising ability to change human hearts?

3. Evaluate: After delivering hard truth to an abuser, you need to give them time and space to consider your words.

Help Abusers With Grace

Recently 159 members of our church completed a survey to help me prepare for a series and book of messages on abuse, and one of the themes that came up often was the idea of grace. While our church family recognized the need for repentance, strong boundaries, and real consequences, they didn't want to act as if grace didn't apply to abusers.

God would agree. Just one verse after addressing oppression and abuse, the prophet Isaiah wrote, **"Though your sins are like scarlet, they shall be as white as snow; though they are red as crimson, they shall be like wool"** (Isaiah 1:18). Yes, abuse is a sin that stains us in ways that we can't wash out. But God can make us clean. Jesus was abused on a cross so that even abusers could be saved. So that you could come to him with all of the consequences and end up with no condemnation. So that God himself could look at you and see someone who brings him joy, someone who has been rescued by Jesus.

Two thousand years ago, our Savior chose Simon the Zealot (a man associated with a violent group of Jewish rebels) and Saul of Tarsus (a religious man who hurt many people) to repent and follow him, proof that grace isn't reserved for good people.

That grace is for you too. Confess your sins to God and others, and believe the good news that grace is for abusers too.

1. Read Acts 9:26-28, thinking through this story through the lens of abuse. Name at least three details of this text that get your attention.

2. How many abusive people will see the face of God in heaven? How does your answer affect the way you treat those same people here on earth?

3. Consider the blessing of prison ministry. If your heart is drawn to sharing grace via letters with a prisoner, research the best way to get involved and be a blessing to those in deep spiritual need.

If You Can Save Just One

As I was preparing to teach a series of messages on abuse, members of our church gave me some honest feedback on a survey about these topics. Many of the responses, comments, and stories gripped my heart, urging me to approach every sermon with humility, truth, and grace. The wounds and trauma and triggers were real, emotional hurts that held on long after the abuse ended.

But one comment caught me more than the others. A woman wrote, "If you can save just one person from the situation they are in, you have done a wonderful thing." Just one person is wonderful.

I wish that our efforts would end every act of abuse once and for all, but this world is too broken for that. Yet Jesus' stories about one lost coin and one lost sheep and one lost son remind us of the celebration in heaven when a single soul is found. When you came to faith in Jesus, the angels didn't mope around in heaven, lamenting the billions of others who hadn't come to faith yet. Instead, they put on their party hats and danced around the throne that you, that "just one," had been saved.

As you seek justice and attempt to help and heal both the abused and the abusers you know, remember this wise woman's words. Just one person matters to God. Just one. **"Learn to do right; seek justice. Defend the oppressed"** (Isaiah 1:17).

1. Another member of our church emailed, "I cannot find the words to express how important this series has been to abuse survivors and those who are still experiencing abuse. To know that our church admits there is a problem and is willing to speak out gives hope that lives can change. I could say thank you a thousand times, and it still would not be enough. You have touched more lives than you will ever know." How does simply admitting there is a problem give hope to the abused?

2. We live in a world that idolizes success and insists on tracking the return on our investments. How do Jesus' stories about the value of a single soul (see Luke 15) critique this common way of looking at life? How will Jesus' worldview shape the way you approach loving others this week?

3. Spend five minutes in prayer for a single person in your life who is hurting in some evident way. Afterward, send them a message and let them know that you were talking to our Father about their future.

Conclusion

I hope that the Bible passages and personal stories in this book have brought some small amount of healing to your soul, no matter what your history with abuse.

Now it's your turn. There are hurting souls out there who need your help. While their stories might be complex, God's plan of restoration will be simple.

Healing = Bible + People.

Resources

Need Help?

1. *Time of Grace* television series *Abuse: What Does God Say?* Find it at timeofgrace.org.

2. Your Pastors—While your pastors are not trained/licensed counselors and should not replace a professional therapist, they are equipped to help you deal with the effects of sin on your soul, including those sins that have been committed against you. Their confidential, Christ-centered guidance can be one vital piece of your recovery and healing.

3. Christian Family Solutions (christianfamilysolutions.org)— CFS is a professional, Christian counseling organization that exists to help and heal people in need. CFS has many licensed counselors on staff who are trained to help individuals who have been abused. CFS clinicians can integrate an individual's Christian faith into therapy so that the healing power of the gospel is present during the treatment process. Appointments are available in person or through telehealth. Call 800.438.1772 for more information.

Websites

1. GRACE (Godly Response to Abuse in the Christian Environment; netgrace.org)—GRACE helps Christian ministries recognize, prevent, and respond to abuse in its various forms. I found this website to be a rich resource of videos and articles for anyone looking for biblical answers on sexual, emotional, verbal, and/or physical abuse.

2. Freedom for the Captives (freedomforcaptives.com)—This ministry was created to help protect children from abuse in

addition to empowering abuse survivors. Filled with Scripture and free resources, Freedom for the Captives is a wonderful place for congregations to learn about how to make their churches safe places for every child to worship Jesus.

Books

1. *Rid of My Disgrace: Hope and Healing for Victims of Sexual Assault* by Justin and Lindsey Holcomb—This was the first book that I ever read on the topic of abuse and, nearly a decade later, continues to be one of my favorites. This work focuses on sexual abuse and guides the reader to the cleansing, purifying, and restoring work of Jesus.

2. *The Body Keeps the Score: Brain, Mind, and Body in the Healing of Trauma* by Bessel van der Kolk—This book, recommended by Dr. Brandon Hayes of Christian Family Solutions, explores the connection between various types of trauma and our brains' ability to trust, practice self-control, and experience pleasure afterward. This pioneering work has become a *New York Times* best seller.

3. *On the Threshold of Hope: Opening the Door to Healing for Survivors of Sexual Abuse* by Diane Mandt Langberg, PhD—This book, recommended by Sheryl Cowling of Christian Family Solutions, is written for men and women who have been traumatized by sexual abuse and approaches healing from a Christian perspective. Cowling has 25 years' experience counseling children, teens, and adults. She is Board Certified as a professional Christian counselor, as an expert in traumatic stress, and in tele-mental health.

About the Writer

Pastor Mike Novotny has served God's people in full-time ministry since 2007 in Madison and, most recently, at The CORE in Appleton, Wisconsin. He also serves as the lead speaker for Time of Grace, where he shares the good news about Jesus through television, print, and online platforms. Mike loves seeing people grasp the depth of God's amazing grace and unstoppable mercy. His wife continues to love him (despite plenty of reasons not to), and his two daughters open his eyes to the love of God for every Christian. When not talking about Jesus or dating his wife/girls, Mike loves playing soccer, running, and reading.

About Time of Grace

Time of Grace is an independent, donor-funded ministry that connects people to God's grace—his love, glory, and power—so they realize the temporary things of life don't satisfy. What brings satisfaction is knowing that because Jesus lived, died, and rose for all of us, we have access to the eternal God—right now and forever.

To discover more, please visit timeofgrace.org or call 800.661.3311.

Help share God's message of grace

Every gift you give helps Time of Grace reach people around the world with the good news of Jesus. Your generosity and prayer support take the gospel of grace to others through our ministry outreach and help them experience a satisfied life as they see God all around them.

Give today at timeofgrace.org/give or by calling 800.661.3311.

Thank you!